GHOST POT

Ghost Pot

John Wedgwood Clarke

Valley Press

First published in 2013 by Valley Press
Woodend, The Crescent, Scarborough, YO11 2PW
www.valleypressuk.com

ISBN: 978-1-908853-27-1
Cat. no.: VP0046

A CIP record for this book is
available from the British Library

Printed and bound in Great Britain by
TJ International Ltd, Padstow, Cornwall

www.valleypressuk.com/authors/johnwedgwoodclarke

Contents

Acknowledgements

Thanks are due to the editors of the following magazines, periodicals and anthologies in which some of these poems first appeared: *Poetry Wales, Fulcrum, The Wolf, Best British Poetry 2012* (Salt), *The Rialto, The Warwick Review, The SHOp, The London Magazine, Oxford Magazine, Poetry Nottingham* and *The Reader.*

'Limpet' was runner-up in the Poetry London Prize 2011; 'Scarborough Elegies' shortlisted for the Manchester Poetry Prize 2010; 'Grey Mullet' won first prize in the Nottingham Open. 'Roman Tear Bottles' won second prize in the Strokestown International Poetry Competition; 'Scarborough Elegies (5)' was displayed on the side of Queen Elizabeth Hall, South Bank, as part of the South Bank Centre's Festival of Britain celebrations, 2011.

A number of poems were written as part of a commission from Chrysalis Arts' Extending Practice/Celebrating Project, which was funded by Arts Council England and Business Link York & North Yorkshire legacy funds. 'Scarborough Moonlight' was commissioned by the Mercer Art Gallery, Harrogate, for their *Atkinson Grimshaw: Painter of Moonlight* exhibition, 2011.

My thanks also to Penny Shuttle and Carol Rumens for their insight and sensitive advice.

for Lara

Ghost Pot

You can't haul this one out. The rope ends
in waves and boulders, in nothing,
after an hour of falling tide; the pot torn free,
bumping along, off in the undertow,
a voracious loss that no one remembers
but you. The bait will make bait
of its catch, an odour so strong,
stones will lift up their arms, claw to be
made flesh, puzzle the shape of death
and find it give way. The caged sea
flows on as they eat from answer
to question, unpacking their hunger,
one to another, until up it comes, a by-catch,
crammed to the throat with bony shields.

Limpet

You only get one shot at me unless
you're armed. Miss, and watch me weep
as I weld to my scar; hit, and I'm loss
in a locket, a bull in a nutshell.
Press my foot as you might dig a thumbnail
into your palm to stop from laughing
at a poem beginning, *dead, lifeless, still...*
hey presto: black speck eyes and a tragic mouth.
As the weight flows I lift on my skirts
and wander the village paths, keeping
them open while the stars rampage.
What measured me has gone. That he, now she,
is me, makes all the difference: our
stones unravel in the pull of the moon.

Periwinkles at Saltwick Bay

All of them moving, bison of the mudstone plain
migrating between shallow pools,
shovel-loads of them, their soft hearts
sealed shut at low tide by a whorled operculum.
The Scar is always about to bloom.
Look closer and it is: they are growing
their promise, flesh secreting colour-
matched stone, buds everywhere stirring
in coral weed, alum shale, sea coal.
We have taken away mountains and still
they return to their harvest of tiny
necessities. In pits where the fool's gold
ammonites have been hacked out
they gather in grey chrysanthemum hoards.

Black Dog Whelk Feeds on a Barnacle

Lost keys run riot between desk and pocket,
leave me for dead at the door.
I won't be sweet: there's a hairline crack
in this sun-baked shell that's lost all faith in the sea.
Black Dog Whelk listens through itself
and every move I fail to make,
aches and drills and knows it's only time
before it thins the dark, a stony light
about to break between table, cup and tap.
I can't say my name and begin and begin.
He's in my throat, his toothed tongue
whispering down long corridors of bone
but no one's here to answer
or speak the crackling emptiness of this room.

Fret

What snapped in you was nearly as hopeful
as the coltsfoot's colonisation of
raw earth, its tell-tale rhizomes piercing clay
baked hard as brick, as if to say all's safe,
this wasting mass is back as land,
begun again with flowers precise as fibre-
optic cables waiting to be spliced, their
pin-prick streams of numbered voices blinded
into yellow silence, replicated,
eyeing everywhere, like the suns of childhood.
The fog cups its hand around each bloom,
listens while it gathers there, replete,
eminently forgetful, as the iron
pleasure steamer ghosts, then turns into the fret.

Cornelian Bay

Alone up here is just too much: let's
stage-dive shingle, tombstone fall,
slam the slab. How it gives. Devils scoured out
in details of sandstone, cornelian, quartz;
glass frosted in its roaring mouth,
in icy voices wolf-whistling
to the inner ear, skinhead flint
shoved into eyes, and bearing them
back to the blood that put them here
where the North Sea sifts and rattles, its finger
on my heart. And as it hands me back,
my face soft-studded with parting kisses,
whoever that was is a shallow scrape,
lost for a moment in crowding light.

Seafarers

As if the ground were flying, the wind
rushes them from under us
into a cloud of cries, the sky a cathedral
of comings and goings, the sea
littered with raptures of spray. Chalk
dazzles their scripture illuminated
with blue netting, straw and guano:
each in its tongue speaks opacity
and joy, turning beyond us in empty
polyphony: fulmar, guillemot
kittiwake, the gannets so close to laughter
the old poem falls into place,
a tourist boat at the white cliff's base
held in the interlace of echo and absence.

Robin Hood's Bay

Between the shadow of the trickling cliff
and rising tide, we scatter among
ammonites our crumbled oatcakes, eggshell,
banana skins coiled in yoghurt pots –
imprints of a family picnic. A slight
swell rustles stippled light through kelp.
The children are opening into the sky,
their rock pool gone tepid with play,
ribs, like hidden gills, slippery under skin.
We have come far, our lives notched
by changing bags, arguments and carriers,
to stand at the water's edge and hear
their voices claim our breath, tighten it
with love, as waves collapse on stone.

Filey Brigg

One-sided in the wind, the other spills
away in grass and kittiwake, leeward
intimacies of wind-curl and thorn-rush,
the old field running its green comb
into a lake by the cliff edge. Gulls
stall furiously trying to land on its silver
teeth. The wind hardens the test.
Molehills melt into baileys, tumuli,
middens, the earth willow-patterned
and silent. In the vast car park, a solitary car
congeals salt on its windscreen,
is tugged a little, the red-shuttered
café in its rear-view like a memory
abandoned after too many visits. The clay
goes on with its gabble, unstoppable.
Again and again the path rewrites
around the problem of gravity, space,
picking its way over ditches and cracks,
tempted by the black-backed gull,
red smoke filling the tide. The Roman
tower is now no more than a signboard
that won't match up with the earth
whose jewellers have worked for days
on a gull. The wind is working still,
whispers about the white rocket-pole, utters
notches, footholds, lost voices, signs
of the way we once spoke to the sea,
to the dark shapes, to the distant us,
our words bright in the crumbling light.

2.

There was never anyone home and nowhere
to knock. Half a kilometre of ice,
a blue-white bone curve,
water and gravel, quiet silt
of spur and valley, the igneous
glitter of mica and rose quartz
graded and resting in twenty metres
of glacial till, no boulders. A far-
reaching stone-cold story
by accident, or mind-numbing
mass-wasting calculation, settled in a cliff
with doors, clay cathedral doors
studded with frost-shattered stones.
Water slips into a footprint.
The OS map melts in mineral sweat,
crumb and slab, the infinite coast
on the move, fractal and fluid,
danger signs in free-fall, posts
flung awry, pipes bone-shattered.
Burrows recoil their blood-space
like soft horns, their holes
piercing the cliff edge. The clay doors
bulge, spill the land's larder
in a largesse of mud: *porridge, butter,*
fois gras, sun-struck chocolate, gut
flab, earth vomitorium…

no echo comes back. The clay
in our words, a level of grist, a hunger
for the first shapes we made
in our mouths, the way we kneaded
and plugged, the way they flowered
entries, sea-anemone blobs,
first rage-houses and love-holds, in-depth
soundings of an arm sleeved in mud,
a stranger's voice taking root in our mouths.

3.

Its two glass discs
missing and knot of
breathing apparatus
gone, we try it on,
the perished black
rubber clutching our
heads in its hand.
We can breathe through
a hole, see through
two holes: we are housed,
anonymous, our voices
swimming in and out
of our mouths,
tentacles with tiny barbs
no matter what we do.
Wave to me, wave
from here where stone
should be, give me
the ok, I'm going under.
Your eyes are on their
own, they shine
in its wreck. That's enough.
Take a picture of this
masked boulder, look
how it looks in the eye.

4.

Behind layers of silence, the sun
is trying to break through, white
voiced and without centre
but enough to give us shadows
we hand in like passports
at the foot of the cliff.
The cold scrutinises, x-rays
our clothes. We are stripped
and led to ourselves, flesh
a stranger we have not
known in years, not like this.
No wind here, but the sound of clinking
halliards rising to a frenzy
over by the yacht club. A coble towers up
onto the beach. It isn't for us.
We open our wind-sealed lips,
scatter rose-hips among
mussel shells, furbelows
with pepper-dulse, each growing
clearer, small differences,
small bridges to things
we agree on being there: *Brigg* –
the sign of a tongue on a pebble.

Sea Buckthorn

Hippophae, glittering horse –
another name
for this stubby North Sea shrub
with olive-like leaves,
fruit more stone than flesh,
at home on motorways
and here, where frost
scallops tideline and colour
gives form the slip,
its berries lifting from thorns
in thin orange smoke
up Tenants Cliff,
the sea tin-lit,
tilting in slightly, anchoring
air, landslip, stripped white trees,
crows grinding out
many centres of the coming night.

Whale

threepence to hear the echo
in the hollow of his cerebellum
– Herman Melville

Your body haunts their measurements:
a finger plugged in the entrance to my ear,
an arm adrift to its pit in my flesh
as it wallowed in search of a source.

They loomed me up, trellis for the wind,
a sublime folly, mildewed, forgotten
on the Long Walk, 'til these ribs broke rank
and they buried my rabble of bones.

Now you've laid me out like an ancestor.
I am washed, between worlds, a cargo
of misshapes, riddled with tiny black holes.
Beneath the geometry of plaster, my spine's

an oar-headed thing of tide and muscle,
seas away from Cerberus at the heel
of Hercules. No one now can enter
my tumbled bone-house. I haunt your body

until our bones are one. I have heard
oceans echo like this hall, cries hung like stars.
Listen for your face – you cannot hear it:
your heart is a skiff in the ocean of mine.

Below the Abbey

1. Who art in heaven

Below Caedmon's song the heavens turn
to stone, and stone-breath, the wounded
tipping from a ship, tipped from their cries,
their letters, dusty boxes, stiff pictures
in another strew of wave on scar,
toothed wrack and hair. Hell is mudstone,
sea anemones and cast-out snakes,
hushed light in the kelp beds, the Abbey
a hollow idea, sieving the wind,
out of sight, its pillars wormy with gaps
a child's finger might search along the edge
of heaven, light pounding into the nave.

2. Gansey

The steps to St Mary's climb up their chests,
each stitch on the five steel pins
lifting the drowned from scar, from tide pool,
from Sandsend and Saltwick,
carrying them up, each stitch knotted breath,
as the box pew stays empty, calling them home.

3. Bioturbation

His memory is snapshot, but for the early days.
How everything was fertile and settled,
smoke and motes in a corridor
of light, words falling from the sky

into miles of listening, burrowing through
into light, the mouth open –
a cold plunge, a long gaze into running water, things
falling into breath, things edging out,

let go in swift currents – the mouth
shaping round whatever the white space brought,
breath fabulous as jellyfish,
a vast skitter of shells blown along in the stream.

4. *The Wreck of the Cretablock*

From the cliff it looks like the sea's abbey,
down here it hides among boulders.
We gather the wreck of the *Cretablock*
as we walk – a bridge, a prow,
the stern a cracked-open groundnut.

How exhausted the world must have been
to set concrete afloat, malleability
churned up and torn by the big guns.
It feels at home down here,
the cold solder of limpet and barnacle

seaming it into the scar, a sentence
cut up and scattered, its body
open from odd angles for the fish to flit
through finding something beyond food
in the shape its portholes make.

5. *Black Nab*

Someone burnt the telephone directory,
cast it in stone: Black Nab is a stub
of illegible numbers and lost addresses.
We clambered over it in search of numbness,

a hangover cure, losing ourselves
as we circled its base on each other's heels,
fatherless actors, conquering sons
risen against the silence between us, singing

it out on a crumbling stage.
                               The old path
by the sewage works has upped sticks
and fallen away. Pigeons pass over
and clear the air. All the old angles of vision

have changed; it could hardly have been here –
the black shale, your distance only the sea.

6. Coal Picker

He's a long way from his stove and keen to talk.
He's a long way from unburdening himself
of a bucket of sea coal. He talks stone
to get it off his chest, a loner in oilskins, doom
merchant, fire in his belly, lava
under a crust of fused tar. His voice
flickers, a spill of town gas. He tells it
like he owns the place, the jet seam, the jewellery
he's made to hang from his wife, his mother.

7. Jet

It flowers in the gloom of museum front rooms:
gingko, snuffbox, fake sepia in a black frame,
whoever's son lost twice over. Lighter than coal,
it floats just enough to avoid getting smashed.

8. *Florilegium*

Overcast light brings out the colour of flowers.
Bring flowers down here. The cliffs
drop tap-roots of ice into earth-shadow.
Bring the sea violet's wild wound,
frenzies of thrift, celandine lit from within.
The cliffs flower darkness, iron,
anaerobic depositions, the pressure
a florilegium of silence we crack open
to view pictures of deaths that no one foretold.

9. Bram Stoker

His ear was extraordinary, as if he'd sucked
the voices from their mouths, given them wings
of their own to go on transfusing life
into brittle bodies, a crypt of shelves.

10. Whitby Fog Signal

The foghorn trumpets listen to waves
in miniature, tinny and tiny
and perfectly *not* waves,
but ghosts of the shoreline filling the ear.

What the black cows make of its bellowing
after the calf of distance
is for another world. Today the sun
makes a painted statue of the racing pigeon

on a ledge below the cliff edge;
swifts, an airy measure of rock fall.
All is clear as hollow-boned hogweed.
Wasps butt one silence up against another.

Marsh Marigold

I listened in to light
and heard its yellow hum:
a tuning fork just struck
and planted on my temple.

It was cold and clear as water
dripping from a glacier,
poised as a hare
a blink away from woods.

Nothing could follow on,
not I, not tomorrow nor
next spring. It paused the air
and screwed it tight as stone.

I listened for as long
as I could bear to think it
perfect, untarnished, a tongue
with nothing to say,

while tiny trills of flies
unzipped ripples from the glaze
of water it vaulted through,
each unfolded flower

an eye annihilating eyes,
a singular harmonic
sprung from the flowing scales
of earth and light and rain.

House

I light fires to cut you adrift in the sky,
leave curtains undrawn to let myself in.

*

From one spindle to the next you play
the wooden harp of your arrival from nowhere.

*

He said to his brother: *heaven is a skylight with snow
falling and no one there to watch it.* I listened.

*

The sofa's procession opens windows in the paintwork.
We are only a bruise away from being a house.

*

What has lost me at the turn of the stairs?
Starlings swarm their thumbprint over the harbour.

*

Inside and outside at the same time: ceiling rose;
blue-white brickwork – I have waited for this view.

*

After what we have done to each other,
when you open you astonish the room I find you in.

*

A light-bulb's reflection, ghost of a pear in the maple –
all evening the foghorn, and now, at last, I hear.

Port Mulgrave

1. Odd Thing

A galleon of inertia,
spiders hoist sails
all over it, children
clambering death:
they catch clouds,
sunlight and listen
to the gaps between things
where loss falls
like a rust flake.

A giant mainspring,
overwound, pulled into
a ribbon of steel rule,
clangs the housing
like a gate to a field
of mattress pyres,
the gutted staithe yielding
cables corroded
into giant ammonites.

The remaining lever,
a chicken drumstick
of flange and rod,
feels in the light for a hand
that fits in a space
like the breach of a gun.
Here's the earth's anxiety
dream, an elongating
and foreshortening,

neither bridge nor ship –
E701E 6059-1 –
a serial number, stressed
by the loss of what happens
next, when what happens
next is light seamlessly
repeating it, the rivets
concealing a hole
in the heart. What flowed

from stone set here:
a broken insect
in an ironstone web,
the last of its species. Rust lifts
paint with cold burning.
Give it time. Weather.
Here is a thing, it grows
in the voice, irreversible
flowerings of a bolt.

2. From mouth to hand to mouth the coble is handed on

and the man and the sea and the beach
make the boat between them.
Nothing has ever been written down.
The man feels the swell
in his arm as he planes the strakes,
the beach under his feet as he sets the keel.

Memorable wood – the maker has gone.
The sun anoints tar and diesel.
The boats become ancestors
beside the black fish sheds, litanies of names
they refuse to forget, or cannot,
for their shapes reinvent themselves like local faces.

So long not afloat, the copper rivets
show proud, outwearing generations of paint;
the skin of hours of days spent under the hull
with caulk, felt and brush,
shrivels without purchase, and the spruce
comes clean, entering into driftwood.

Here, where everlasting plastics
everlast, continue to contain
rainwater, ODIN on his perished cradle
dreams a tombstone fish box: *Sea Fresh*, Eyemouth.

3. Bait Shed

Square-corrugated sheeting
they use for industrial estates
has been cut into a shed that stands out
like a sawn up caravan
among wooden improvisations.
This dwelling frames no view.
How you get into its dark is what matters:
a driftwood arbour,
with inflatable life-jackets
like large wineskins
hung from stripped branches,
leads to a Romanesque buffalo skull-arch
over a door with driftwood tusks.
Outside is dangerous with silence.
There are many people in there
and no one. Behind the shed
the shale cliff rises like a wave.

Huggate

Their names are mouthfuls of water
we pass down the line –
musk thistle, cock's foot, red fescue –
until the hedgerow stutters
into an abyss of barley,
a river of seed and clashing awn.

In distant lay-bys, our memories
fade in sun-stricken cars
like old postcards on a market stall
we sent to reassure ourselves,
only the other day, we knew
where we were, could name our love.

A crow stakes a tree on the other side
of the rippling valley, each call
a chalky gash in the constellations
of trefoil and moss, through which the dead
wade out to cool our feet
and drink the words from our mouths.

Burnet Rose

I've never been able to breathe deeply enough
to reach the source of your scent.
While you speak, every pink remark
is the case; but they pass like butterflies
in shining eddies.
                          Speak for me,
your stem, wild with green static
electricity I just have to earth. I pull you
towards me again and find your anthers
like rags of old christening robes,
and curled at the fountain's base,
an earwig, pollen-dusted, welcome
at last in the petal-light of homecoming.

Sleeping Child

You sleep, while names of villages rise
and fall away, tail-lights dwindling ahead
until only we summon the sign
for crossing deer, steer by the constellation
of a pub. The edges where the wipers
shove the rain gel and tremble, sucked thin
by small riptides. I rest my elbow on
the door-frame like my father would and read
the road through fingertips. A milestone
unfolds, lets go of the verge, the barn owl
gone before I realise – that's how we get home.
And what will you recall of the sudden lift
from car to bed, your eyes broken open
for a moment by the light in the hall?

Lightships

The trawler crawls in
with night on its shoulders,
wings folded
in glittering holds.

Around the harbour
we talk our way
into the dark hatchings
of lobster pots.

We have reached one of many
points. The boat slides
between stone.
The lightships scatter and let go.

Scarborough Elegies

1. Sandside

Don't go: light rises up before the gull,
the fishing's good. Lower the orange line,
listen to the shallows as a crab
plays arpeggios on the mud piano,
his touch like someone picking stitches.
It's hopeless here: the tide falls,
absence stinks; no forgetting
you're coming and going. If a brick falls
it stays fallen, sparrows flit through
lobster pots and all boats shatter the sky.
A boy mimics the gulls, head flung back
gagging on air, regurgitating life
in a sound like raw sea light, its stone buds
opening, a sign of nothing but flight.

2. Otter boards

Once a trawl begins, water pressure
drags apart the Otter boards and the foot rope
rumbles up a dust storm, the sea
woken mid-dream, familiar words gone strange

in its mouth, uttered and sound-bitten,
their habitats erased, or clenched back in
turbid ruins. Beside the tank of diesel,
the ice house and heaps of chain, the stacked boards

say nothing they've seen, material
silence, gathering rust at the harbour mouth.

3. Historic Diving Society

By the lighthouse, a mighty thrush
has been hard at it since dawn:
many bronze snail shells litter the pier,
pierced and glazed over, the damage
crisscrossed by brass threads,
watch-glass windows. Diving suits, crucified
upside down against the white wall,
leak bodies, hair dragged and shoved back
under, monstrous scabs of pearl.
A wooden box like a *What-the-*
Butler-Saw, with two handle-wheels to strip
a man to breath, bellows down the air
into a globe-like shell, where someone
fumbles, his hands like two disasters.

4. *Lighthouse*

The lighthouses have lost their way:
after the bombardment, only the memory
of light, the replica lantern room
like an old-fashioned birdcage
at an auction house, the bird long gone
singing its horizon on forgotten frequencies.

5. *Outer Harbour*

Low tide in the outer harbour – a distant transmission
from the North Sea rolls in across the shining mud
like the raised veins on the back of a mother's hand,

transparent veins from a cloudy body always
there and unmemorable, a gaze gone quiet and present,
in which it marks its first return, tiredness

dilating into life, message breaking without air,
no bright reflection but refraction, a magnification of mud
that travels between the gravestones of bare keels.

We've prepared for her return, children offering up
our secret weight: a net, a flag, some fuel, lifebuoys –
all going nowhere, waiting for her touch to lighten us.

6. No Letting Go

Salmon Steps, Long Greece Steps, the steps
down a mine, down the side of a wreck,
down a ship, down your first house,
your last, down the side of a pier,
here, where a nail's been abandoned
by the wood around it, its stubborn song
banging on out of childhood. First nail
of summer, thumb and hammer,
the return of the banging, precision of rage,
the thumb and the hammer, the belt
and the whys and wherefores of song,
this measurable portion, the rule
on the rough stones for depth of the water,
for the moon-made numbers, for low-tide haunting,
high tide clarities, and whatever the tide,
fathoming what's left, the numerals
enveloped, revealed, chiselled or painted,
as toothed rack drifts past like an astronaut
cut from his craft, heading for deep space.

7. Castle Headland

Down below, a pocket garden
of neon seed heads,
above, a levitating meadow
steps off into air –

up here, all scale is reversed:
a haphazard samba
of crickets measures its song
around me, out-trilling

Thriller. Flakes of snail trail
persist on stone chips
like the remnants of a language
spoken by night –

ants are wild in the heat
dismantling it in the
absence of anything else
to carry off, just the odd noun

left shining the history
of a hidden mouth. The bay is filled
with small boats caught
in wet paint, the stones afloat.

A host of black gnats jostles,
tiny tumblers dizzying the path
that rises to the walls,
patched and broken walls

coming and going, as they do.
How little I know of
the clouds that have come
to gaze at the edge of the land.

Grey Mullet

Their mouths were small, lips too soft
to tether a run, or bear their weight
when hoisted up by hook alone.
I never owned a landing net, but read the book
and rolled the crumb of bread
into a seed of dough that hid the hook.
Sometimes the bait would dance
like a table at a séance, until it fell away,
eclipsed. More often, they just hovered
by the steps, around green chains,
scaling the distance between boat and shadow,
oblivious, as if they listened out
for someone to arrive, enthralled
by a sound on the edge of their hearing.

Cloughton Wyke

1.

Iron light. Fulmar and kittiwake
laugh in Anglo-Saxon,
ripple quick shadows
over the beach.

There are roots
in rock, charcoal sticks
in split sandstone
where waves beat the cliff.

Facing east, a slab of Jurassic beach,
wedged end-on,
nurses wave-echo
above its rippled surface.

2.

Not an *umbrageous grot*,
but a sop of grass streaming rain
down the cliff,

a bower of water-spatter, moment's
mineral bliss,
a pebble in the hollow it's shaped.

Mud fronds and seawater
tangle and merge
as the tide guzzles in.

Down the centre of the Wyke
gulls have gathered
in a hesitant line: summer starts here,

elbowing into cliffs.
A black flag leans
in the stiff north-easterly wind.

Pillbox, Cayton Bay

Desire's beeline finds them out, no matter
how grass hazes or brambles entangle,
and enters among their introverted
lighthouse beams to stand within a secret buzz,
listen out across a view to die for.
But not this: the clay has given way,
left a concrete, cliff-top corridor
teetering like a train carriage, and slid the pillbox
over and down to the beach, then melted
away: a foursquare boulder adrift.
Sharp turn, and you're in breath's oratory,
thronged and hurled by other air,
walking on a ceiling ribbed with sand,
the loopholes jammed with wet, black stones.

South Batts

Seabirds have left the auditorium littered
with silence composing itself.
All along the path
ladybirds bejewel warm silver fence posts.

The cliff edge magnifies each movement towards it –
the orange buoy, tide-unfolding snags,
space so meticulous
it is impossible to see the way between here and when.

Sunday Painter

A stone like a half-pan of watercolour
the brush has worked at
to make a stone like a half-pan of watercolour
the brush has worked at hard.
There is everything here for the land to paint itself.
It absorbs the light as it comes in,
an anechoic light-chamber in which rust sings
and winter purples vermillion pantiles.
Test the eye and find the stone flow through the arm
like a rock in a stream.
A hymn is beginning to sing in the white ground.
Tide has risen and brushes a suitcase,
brushes brushes like a stand of trees
growing from the sand, their tips
slurried with colours, buttery commingling of the time
it has taken to lift over pebbles,
filling spaces between marks with buoyancy, breath.
So many pictures get in the way.
So many arms enter the arm and guide it away from the eye
and the stone. The brush is an umber flame:
let it burn through the eye and into kelp fields.
The hymn sings itself and the brush fears not.
The Sabbath stones open themselves like chapels.

Scarborough Moonlight

after Atkinson Grimshaw

The moon makes consciousness a lamp:
all the Old Town glows
with voices the moon defines –
yellow winter pub-talk clacking down wet steps;
red arcades arguing in waves;
colours gone inwards, knowing limits
as the moon soaks castle and terrace,
outcrop and mausoleum.

The moon studies the town as a large-format negative:
it tells no one, gathers everything,
burrows deeper in the eye
than the sun, fish-cold, and finds the mind
scumbling, a painter, speculative
waiting to welcome the boat in a smudge,
the name of the night in hog hair and pigment,
to coat a ghost-glass with flesh.

It is patient beyond the moon itself,
waits for the click of a switch to pour in
its plaster-of-Paris, to castaway hallway and landing
in the stare of a skylight,
a gaze so solid, so open, our bodies unfold
in its eye, breath a landscape
in the lungs, bottled in a dark car
above Holbeck landslip.

The moon empties childhood from the playground
in Castle Dykes for the fox
to slip again from the scrub, angel of the moon,
baulks and bolts filling as it glides
through riggings of thorn,
over ants' nests and thistle-navels,
marking trees of lead lettering in Paradise,
gone in the fish-nerve of rain down Tuthill.

The moon gives Castle Headland a wet beating,
silvers the seed-head
of St. Mary's clock face,
illuminates all that trickles and spills
through channel and pool,
the scar's dark riddled with returning water.
The sea listens, umbrella furled,
drawn by the light to losses it cannot place.

Salt Pans

Your camera holds me kindly
and bids me come into its room.

I thank it for its hospitality and leave
someone to remind me I was never there.

He repays the debt for me by setting up home.
Whenever I visit, he will not let me in.

He, alone, remembers my grandmother's voice
and the scent of those matchboxes.

Yesterday your camera placed his voice
in the mouth of a man who gazes at limpets

by The Salt Pans as if they were roses
on old pink wallpaper, his hidden gaze

a constellation of cambric bedroom light.
He kissed the fingers that made the shutter close.

Roman Tear Bottles

Tiny pockets of puff, fragile as yolks
at the lips of jugs, they spin from themselves
capillaries of light, fluent risks,
each body's green-blue abdomen
a memory of streams, milky iridescence.
What they hold was always gone
and so they measure it with craft, their throats
teased out, thirsty for our eyes,
their tiny handles offering the kiss
of thumb and forefinger, the scale of grief.
Repeated, beyond repetition, they tilt
on a paradigm of glass, each one
a catch of breath, transparency prickled
with tiny bubbles, a nettle rash of light.

Dark Rooms

before I am lost
hell must open like a red rose
for the dead to pass
– H.D.

1. Runswick Duck Pond

Dry bread and bones in the head
of a sleeping mallard, dry hands and Mother's
Pride in the tread of the walker
passing like a shade along the path by the pond
at the cliff edge as one eye opens,
a spiracle in black velvet, confirming another
walker passing in search
of a voice that says stop, here
is where we feed the ducks, the end
of our walk, mind your fingers, throw it
far, or crumble it near, they'll come yammering,
hungry for ghosts of bread
that bloom as they sink. Dry bread and bones,
my hands pointless without your play.

2. Kettleness

I had a little egg timer, nothing would it bear.
I had a little song, and everything it bore.
When I danced, all the birds of the air,
all the silver in the sun
that ghosts the world at noon
glittered through that egg-timer.
I turned and I turned it, a tightening
in the throat, and everything it bore,
a little heap of pale-blue grains, passing
into noon.
           Wild cuts the solitary bee makes
between dead-nettle and vetch,
daylight seals shut. Fetch a pail of icy water.
Larks fall to hay meadow as ash.
Look back, Kettleness is hourglass dust.

3. *Wild Camping*

Wind-worried, a black mermaid's purse
pegged by the path, an interior
he twitches in like a day-lit embryo.
He wakes inside, a fading print of himself.
He's forgotten how to look at her
and looks to make sure she's there.
But she's gone, zipping him in,
too hot, shivering him away
in a skitter of cold stones down her spine,
finding the rippled, ancient meadow,
a green-orange-purple rainbow
of stalk, flag and seed-head. She rubs her hip,
sore from another night turning
on the dry earth until it gave her exit.

4. Wrack Hills

A yellow door in the grass by the edge of the field.
Land-simmer. Horses veined like leaves.
Aggressive wheat. Half thought, half
moment of the world, freighters
mark time in haze, their containers packed
with polystyrene seed, everlasting ties.
The path goes down in shade.
Beneath snuffed blackthorn the bramble
flowers open like swimmers
breaking surface, before diving again
into dark-eyed rooms, flavour condensed
from breath the size of summer
held for a voice behind hedgerows calling
through the evening field, calling in the seeded shoes.

5. Lingrow Knock

Don't worry, the gulls say, that tilt and hold
below the linear progress of the plane.
Here's the cliff, and the wind comes to us.
The greater plantain wears a crown of creamy anthers.
The fishing boat wears a tumbling crown of gulls.
An ant skates over the path
like a needle on a smooth record.
Idle speech on the wind lets loose
words through air to the stirring of water
over Lingrow Knock, elderflower-champagne air,
shadows poured from bright nibs
of sandstone. We are never near and far,
only between, dwellers on the updraft,
stone and sea-breath clear in our cries.

6. Lingrow Cliffs

A man strides by in a Lycra suit of armour,
life clenched between his jaws
for fear of dropping. Another with straws
taped to his chest, instant hydration,
a walking life-support victim with ski-poles,
running from illness in a dream
the path flickers out into air, a vague
serpent, every rise swelling silence,
a sheep's jawbone resting by the cliff edge.
All the women are behind them, in them,
as they hunt a song of footsteps, stamping
ants that glide from the cracks
in the packed-earth path like 4am fear –
now, only the relentless biting of the air.

7. Lingrow Howe

There's so much to look at. We stop to admire
the tedder whipping hay into creamy piles,
the bailer spin plastic around
long rooms of hay, like a spider mummifying a fly.
The Howe has been ploughed out
and nothing remains online about finds,
the land divided by wire fences.
Chicken dung smoulders all day by the long shed,
the small stone barn filled with Topwrap
by Veloc. Who has roots here?
Only the eyes as they touch the cut sward.
That corner where a horse frisked behind the hedge,
louder, the ground thumped –
I lost my thought, the world coming home.

8. Boulby Mine

The mine is an Escher print of cones, cubes,
cylinders, conveyers, all on the rise
and falling, tiny-windowed,
an Anglo-Saxon monastery. I mine me
and am I we, there are so many walking here
linked by the same feet falling forward
onto the path, voices rattling around
like a hawthorn hedge in the blast
of the same voice, until the gorgeous crow
like my head blown off, unwraps
a flying shelter of sky. In the black meadows
of harvested minerals, *a quiet place
in the universe*, the core of everything
may show itself in a pure coil of light, or not.

9. Skinningrove

The cliffs below the steel mill, Mt Rushmore
as Bacon might have done it –
a thin thread of the Gortex clad makes its way
past windows green with damp.

A young couple from the sea front
one-up-one-downs, drop a plastic tube
into the beck across the road.
The grove remembers itself, not on information boards

or through fibreglass fishermen, but the shine
of brake discs, clutches of scrap and pigeon lofts,
Jede nacht traume, ich von dir stencilled
on vast steel gates rammed open,

and *Townie, I'm gonna get your car*
on a wall at the end of a pier out of *Stalker*
and a good ten-minute walk from the car
if I'd had one. Many grievances of rust

have fractured the concrete – the place is in pieces.
At the end of the pier a door to a building,
a cage of girders, no floors, a lattice
of dares. Maybe iron ore rumbled through it

into holds? It's a puzzle no one needs
to answer, is answered by hollow wing-claps,
the swell clanging iron, and a man who
spins from behind, a man at the end of the pier

hand to mouth, as if flung out
who runs back and flings out again, staggering
back, high in the stone day, a ghost
sun rusting, echoing stone in a scrapyard.

Whitestone Light

From the cliff-top path
I have glimpsed
in the squat tower
a hive of green stillness,

breath without shadow,
the face shoaling
to an impulse not its own
and closed to the public.